Word Count Tracker

for Self-Publishing Authors

eDiY Biz Tools

eDiY Publishing

Writing Projects Master List

	Working Title	Finished
1		☐
2		☐
3		☐
4		☐
5		☐
6		☐
7		☐
8		☐
9		☐
10		☐
11		☐
12		☐
13		☐
14		☐
15		☐
16		☐
17		☐
18		☐
19		☐
20		☐
21		☐
22		☐
23		☐
24		☐
25		☐

Writing Projects Master List

	Working Title	Finished
26	_____	☐
27	_____	☐
28	_____	☐
29	_____	☐
30	_____	☐
31	_____	☐
32	_____	☐
33	_____	☐
34	_____	☐
35	_____	☐
36	_____	☐
37	_____	☐
38	_____	☐
39	_____	☐
40	_____	☐
41	_____	☐
42	_____	☐
43	_____	☐
44	_____	☐
45	_____	☐
46	_____	☐
47	_____	☐
48	_____	☐
49	_____	☐
50	_____	☐

Writing Projects Master List

	Working Title	Finished
51		☐
52		☐
53		☐
54		☐
55		☐
56		☐
57		☐
58		☐
59		☐
60		☐
61		☐
62		☐
63		☐
64		☐
65		☐
66		☐
67		☐
68		☐
69		☐
70		☐
71		☐
72		☐
73		☐
74		☐
75		☐

Word Count
Tracking

Project Type _____

Working Title _____

Date Started ____ / ____ / ____   **Date Completed** ____ / ____ / ____

File Location _____

Date	Time			Word Count	
	Start	Finish	Total	Start	Finish
		Total			Total

Word Count Goal _____ words   **Final Word Count** _____ words

Final Title _____

Final SubTitle _____

_____

_____

Total	Session Notes				

Project Type _____

Working Title _____

Date Started ____ / ____ / ____   **Date Completed** ____ / ____ / ____

File Location _____

Date	Time			Word Count	
	Start	Finish	Total	Start	Finish
		Total			Total

Word Count Goal _____ words **Final Word Count** _____ words

Final Title _____

Final SubTitle _____

_____

_____

Total	Session Notes				

 Continued on page: _____

Project Type _____

Working Title _____

Date Started ___ / ___ / ___   **Date Completed** ___ / ___ / ___

File Location _____

Date	Time			Word Count	
	Start	Finish	Total	Start	Finish
			Total			Total

3

Word Count Goal _____ words **Final Word Count** _____ words

Final Title _____

Final SubTitle _____

_____

_____

Total	Session Notes				

Continued on page: _____

Project Type _____

Working Title _____

Date Started ____ / ____ / ____ **Date Completed** ____ / ____ / ____

File Location _____

Date		Time			Word Count	
	Start	Finish	Total	Start	Finish
			Total			Total

Word Count Goal _____ words **Final Word Count** _____ words

Final Title _____

Final SubTitle _____

_____

_____

Total	Session Notes				

 Continued on page: _____

Project Type _____

Working Title _____

Date Started ___ / ___ / ___   **Date Completed** ___ / ___ / ___

File Location _____

	Time			Word Count	
Date	Start	Finish	Total	Start	Finish
			Total		Total

Word Count Goal _____ words   **Final Word Count** _____ words

Final Title _____

Final SubTitle _____

_____

_____

Total	Session Notes				

 Continued on page: _____

Project Type _____

Working Title _____

Date Started ____ / ____ / ____ **Date Completed** ____ / ____ / ____

File Location _____

	Time			Word Count	
Date	**Start**	**Finish**	**Total**	**Start**	**Finish**
			Total		Total

Word Count Goal _____ words   **Final Word Count** _____ words
Final Title _____
Final SubTitle _____
_____
_____

Total	Session Notes				

Continued on page: _____

Project Type _____

Working Title _____

Date Started ____ / ____ / ____   **Date Completed** ____ / ____ / ____

File Location _____

	Time			Word Count	
Date	**Start**	**Finish**	**Total**	**Start**	**Finish**
			Total		Total

Word Count Goal _____ words **Final Word Count** _____ words

Final Title _____

Final SubTitle _____

_____

_____

Total	Session Notes				

   Continued on page: _____

Project Type _____

Working Title _____

Date Started ____ / ____ / ____   **Date Completed** ____ / ____ / ____

File Location _____

Date	Time			Word Count	
	Start	Finish	Total	Start	Finish
			Total		Total

Word Count Goal _____ words **Final Word Count** _____ words
Final Title _____
Final SubTitle _____

_____

_____

Total	Session Notes				

 Continued on page: _____

Project Type _____

Working Title _____

Date Started ___ / ___ / ___   **Date Completed** ___ / ___ / ___

File Location _____

Date		Time				Word Count
	Start	Finish	Total		Start	Finish
			Total			Total

Word Count Goal _____ words **Final Word Count** _____ words
Final Title _____
Final SubTitle _____

_____
_____

Total	Session Notes				

 Continued on page: _____

Project Type _____

Working Title _____

Date Started ____ / ____ / ____   **Date Completed** ____ / ____ / ____

File Location _____

| Date | Time | | | Word Count | |
	Start	Finish	Total	Start	Finish
		Total			Total

Word Count Goal _____ words **Final Word Count** _____ words

Final Title _____

Final SubTitle _____

_____

_____

Total	Session Notes				

 Continued on page: _____

Project Type _____

Working Title _____

Date Started ____ / ____ / ____   **Date Completed** ____ / ____ / ____

File Location _____

| Date | Time | | | Word Count | |
	Start	Finish	Total	Start	Finish
		Total			Total

Word Count Goal _____ words   **Final Word Count** _____ words

Final Title _____

Final SubTitle _____

_____

_____

Total	Session Notes				

Project Type _____

Working Title _____

Date Started ____ / ____ / ____   **Date Completed** ____ / ____ / ____

File Location _____

Date	Time			Word Count	
	Start	Finish	Total	Start	Finish
			Total		Total

12

Word Count Goal _____ words **Final Word Count** _____ words
Final Title _____
Final SubTitle _____

_____
_____

Total	Session Notes				

Continued on page: _____

Project Type _____

Working Title _____

Date Started ___ / ___ / ___   **Date Completed** ___ / ___ / ___

File Location _____

Date	Time			Word Count	
	Start	**Finish**	**Total**	**Start**	**Finish**
			Total			Total

Word Count Goal _____ words **Final Word Count** _____ words

Final Title _____

Final SubTitle _____

_____

_____

Total	Session Notes				

  Continued on page: _____

Project Type _____

Working Title _____

Date Started ___ / ___ / ___   **Date Completed** ___ / ___ / ___

File Location _____

| Date | Time | | | Word Count | |
	Start	Finish	Total	Start	Finish
			Total			Total

Word Count Goal _____ words   **Final Word Count** _____ words

Final Title _____

Final SubTitle _____

_____

_____

Total	Session Notes				

Continued on page: _____

Project Type _____

Working Title _____

Date Started ____ / ____ / ____   **Date Completed** ____ / ____ / ____

File Location _____

Date	Time			Word Count	
	Start	Finish	Total	Start	Finish
			Total		Total

Word Count Goal _____ words **Final Word Count** _____ words
Final Title _____
Final SubTitle _____

_____
_____

Total	Session Notes				

 Continued on page: _____

Project Type _____

Working Title _____

Date Started ____ / ____ / ____   **Date Completed** ____ / ____ / ____

File Location _____

Date	Time			Word Count	
	Start	Finish	Total	Start	Finish
			Total		Total

Word Count Goal _____ words **Final Word Count** _____ words

Final Title _____

Final SubTitle _____

_____

_____

Total	Session Notes				

 Continued on page: _____

Project Type _____

Working Title _____

Date Started ____ / ____ / ____   **Date Completed** ____ / ____ / ____

File Location _____

| Date | Time | | | Word Count | |
	Start	Finish	Total	Start	Finish
		Total			Total

Word Count Goal _____ words **Final Word Count** _____ words

Final Title _____

Final SubTitle _____

_____

_____

Total	Session Notes				

 Continued on page: _____

Project Type _____

Working Title _____

Date Started ____ / ____ / ____   **Date Completed** ____ / ____ / ____

File Location _____

Date	Time			Word Count	
	Start	Finish	Total	Start	Finish
			Total		Total

Word Count Goal _____ words   **Final Word Count** _____ words

Final Title _____

Final SubTitle _____

_____

_____

Total	Session Notes				

 Continued on page: _____

Project Type _____

Working Title _____

Date Started ____ / ____ / ____   **Date Completed** ____ / ____ / ____

File Location _____

Date	Time			Word Count	
	Start	Finish	Total	Start	Finish
			Total		Total

Word Count Goal _____ words **Final Word Count** _____ words

Final Title _____

Final SubTitle _____

_____

_____

Total	Session Notes				

 Continued on page: _____

Project Type _____

Working Title _____

Date Started ____ / ____ / ____   **Date Completed** ____ / ____ / ____

File Location _____

| Date | Time | | | Word Count | |
	Start	Finish	Total	Start	Finish
		Total			Total

Word Count Goal _____ words **Final Word Count** _____ words

Final Title _____

Final SubTitle _____

_____

_____

Total	Session Notes				

 Continued on page: _____

Project Type _____

Working Title _____

Date Started ___ / ___ / ___   **Date Completed** ___ / ___ / ___

File Location _____

| Date | Time | | | Word Count | |
	Start	Finish	Total	Start	Finish
		Total			Total

Word Count Goal _____ words **Final Word Count** _____ words

Final Title _____

Final SubTitle _____

_____

_____

Total	Session Notes				

 Continued on page: _____

Project Type _____

Working Title _____

Date Started ____ / ____ / ____   **Date Completed** ____ / ____ / ____

File Location _____

Date	Time			Word Count	
	Start	**Finish**	**Total**	**Start**	**Finish**
			Total			Total

Word Count Goal _____ words **Final Word Count** _____ words

Final Title _____

Final SubTitle _____

_____

_____

Total	Session Notes				

Continued on page: _____

Project Type _____

Working Title _____

Date Started ____ / ____ / ____   **Date Completed** ____ / ____ / ____

File Location _____

_____

Date	Time			Word Count	
	Start	Finish	Total	Start	Finish
			Total		Total

Word Count Goal _____ words **Final Word Count** _____ words

Final Title _____

Final SubTitle _____

_____

_____

Total	Session Notes				

  Continued on page: _____

Project Type _____

Working Title _____

Date Started ____ / ____ / ____   **Date Completed** ____ / ____ / ____

File Location _____

	Time			Word Count	
Date	**Start**	**Finish**	**Total**	**Start**	**Finish**
			Total			Total

Word Count Goal _____ words **Final Word Count** _____ words
Final Title _____
Final SubTitle _____

_____
_____

Total	Session Notes				

Project Type _____

Working Title _____

Date Started ____ / ____ / ____   **Date Completed** ____ / ____ / ____

File Location _____

Date	Time			Word Count	
	Start	Finish	Total	Start	Finish
			Total		Total

Word Count Goal _____ words   **Final Word Count** _____ words

Final Title _____

Final SubTitle _____

_____

_____

Total	Session Notes				

51

Continued on page: _____

Project Type _____

Working Title _____

Date Started ____ / ____ / ____   **Date Completed** ____ / ____ / ____

File Location _____

	Time			Word Count	
Date	**Start**	**Finish**	**Total**	**Start**	**Finish**
			Total		Total

Word Count Goal _____ words   **Final Word Count** _____ words
Final Title _____
Final SubTitle _____

_____
_____

Total	Session Notes				

   Continued on page: _____

Project Type _____

Working Title _____

Date Started ___ / ___ / ___   **Date Completed** ___ / ___ / ___

File Location _____

| Date | Time | | | Word Count | |
	Start	Finish	Total	Start	Finish
		Total			Total

Word Count Goal _____ words   **Final Word Count** _____ words

Final Title _____

Final SubTitle _____

_____

_____

Total	Session Notes				

 Continued on page: _____

Project Type   _____

Working Title   _____

Date Started   ____ / ____ / ____   **Date Completed**   ____ / ____ / ____

File Location   _____

	Time			Word Count	
Date	**Start**	**Finish**	**Total**	**Start**	**Finish**
			Total			Total

Word Count Goal _____ words **Final Word Count** _____ words
Final Title _____
Final SubTitle _____

_____
_____

Total	Session Notes				

 Continued on page: _____

Project Type _____

Working Title _____

Date Started ____ / ____ / ____   **Date Completed** ____ / ____ / ____

File Location _____

Date	Time			Word Count	
	Start	Finish	Total	Start	Finish
			Total		Total

Word Count Goal _____ words **Final Word Count** _____ words

Final Title _____

Final SubTitle _____

_____

_____

Total	Session Notes				

Continued on page: _____

Project Type _____

Working Title _____

Date Started ____ / ____ / ____   **Date Completed** ____ / ____ / ____

File Location _____

	Time			Word Count	
Date	**Start**	**Finish**	**Total**	**Start**	**Finish**
			Total			Total

Word Count Goal _____ words   **Final Word Count** _____ words

Final Title _____

Final SubTitle _____

_____

_____

Total	Session Notes				

Continued on page: _____

Project Type _____

Working Title _____

Date Started ____ / ____ / ____   **Date Completed** ____ / ____ / ____

File Location _____

| Date | Time | | | Word Count | |
	Start	Finish	Total	Start	Finish
			Total		Total

Word Count Goal _____ words   **Final Word Count** _____ words

Final Title _____

Final SubTitle _____

_____

_____

Total	Session Notes				

Continued on page: _____

Project Type _____

Working Title _____

Date Started ___ / ___ / ___   **Date Completed** ___ / ___ / ___

File Location _____

| Date | Time | | | Word Count | |
	Start	Finish	Total	Start	Finish
		Total			Total

Word Count Goal _____ words   **Final Word Count** _____ words
Final Title _____
Final SubTitle _____
_____
_____

Total	Session Notes				

 Continued on page: _____

Project Type _____

Working Title _____

Date Started ____ / ____ / ____   **Date Completed** ____ / ____ / ____

File Location _____

	Time			Word Count	
Date	**Start**	**Finish**	**Total**	**Start**	**Finish**
			Total		Total

Word Count Goal _____ words   **Final Word Count** _____ words

Final Title _____

Final SubTitle _____

_____

_____

Total	Session Notes				

 Continued on page: _____

Project Type _____

Working Title _____

Date Started ____ / ____ / ____   **Date Completed**   ____ / ____ / ____

File Location _____

Date	Time			Word Count	
	Start	Finish	Total	Start	Finish
		Total			Total

Word Count Goal _____ words **Final Word Count** _____ words

Final Title _____

Final SubTitle _____

_____

_____

Total	Session Notes				

 Continued on page: _____

Project Type _____

Working Title _____

Date Started ____ / ____ / ____   **Date Completed** ____ / ____ / ____

File Location _____

Date	Time			Word Count	
	Start	**Finish**	**Total**	**Start**	**Finish**
		Total			Total

Word Count Goal _____ words   **Final Word Count** _____ words

Final Title _____

Final SubTitle _____

_____

_____

Total	Session Notes				

   Continued on page: _____

Project Type _____

Working Title _____

Date Started ____ / ____ / ____ **Date Completed** ____ / ____ / ____

File Location _____

| Date | Time | | | Word Count | |
	Start	Finish	Total	Start	Finish
		Total			Total

Word Count Goal _____ words   **Final Word Count** _____ words

Final Title _____

Final SubTitle _____

_____

_____

Total	**Session Notes**				

    Continued on page: _____

Project Type _____

Working Title _____

Date Started ____ / ____ / ____   **Date Completed** ____ / ____ / ____

File Location _____

Date	Time			Word Count	
	Start	Finish	Total	Start	Finish
		Total			Total

Word Count Goal _____ words   **Final Word Count** _____ words

Final Title _____

Final SubTitle _____

_____

_____

Total	Session Notes				

 Continued on page: _____

Project Type _____

Working Title _____

Date Started ____ / ____ / ____   **Date Completed** ____ / ____ / ____

File Location _____

| Date | Time | | | Word Count | |
	Start	Finish	Total	Start	Finish
			Total		Total

Word Count Goal _____ words   **Final Word Count** _____ words
Final Title _____
Final SubTitle _____

_____
_____

Total	Session Notes				

 Continued on page: _____

Project Type _____

Working Title _____

Date Started ____ / ____ / ____ **Date Completed** ____ / ____ / ____

File Location _____

Date	Time			Word Count	
	Start	Finish	Total	Start	Finish
			Total		Total

39

Word Count Goal _____ words   **Final Word Count** _____ words

Final Title _____

Final SubTitle _____

_____

_____

Total	Session Notes				

Project Type _____

Working Title _____

Date Started ____ / ____ / ____   **Date Completed** ____ / ____ / ____

File Location _____

Date	Time			Word Count	
	Start	**Finish**	**Total**	**Start**	**Finish**
			Total		Total

Word Count Goal _____ words **Final Word Count** _____ words

Final Title _____

Final SubTitle _____

_____

_____

Total	Session Notes				

 Continued on page: _____

Project Type _____

Working Title _____

Date Started ____ / ____ / ____   **Date Completed** ____ / ____ / ____

File Location _____

| Date | Time | | | Word Count | |
	Start	Finish	Total	Start	Finish
			Total		Total

Word Count Goal _____ words **Final Word Count** _____ words

Final Title _____

Final SubTitle _____

_____

_____

Total	Session Notes				

 Continued on page: _____

Project Type _____

Working Title _____

Date Started ____ / ____ / ____   **Date Completed** ____ / ____ / ____

File Location _____

| Date | Time | | | Word Count | |
	Start	Finish	Total	Start	Finish
		Total			Total

Word Count Goal _____ words   **Final Word Count** _____ words

Final Title _____

Final SubTitle _____

_____

_____

Total	Session Notes				

 Continued on page: _____

Project Type _____

Working Title _____

Date Started ___ / ___ / ___   **Date Completed** ___ / ___ / ___

File Location _____

Date	Time			Word Count	
	Start	Finish	Total	Start	Finish
			Total		Total

Word Count Goal _____ words **Final Word Count** _____ words
Final Title _____
Final SubTitle _____

_____
_____

Total	Session Notes				

 Continued on page: _____

Project Type _____

Working Title _____

Date Started ____ / ____ / ____ **Date Completed** ____ / ____ / ____

File Location _____

Date	Time			Word Count	
	Start	Finish	Total	Start	Finish
			Total		Total

Word Count Goal _____ words   **Final Word Count** _____ words

Final Title _____

Final SubTitle _____

_____

_____

Total	Session Notes				

 Continued on page: _____

Project Type _____

Working Title _____

Date Started ____ / ____ / ____   **Date Completed** ____ / ____ / ____

File Location _____

| Date | Time | | | Word Count | |
	Start	Finish	Total	Start	Finish
			Total		Total

Word Count Goal _____ words **Final Word Count** _____ words

Final Title _____

Final SubTitle _____

_____

_____

Total	Session Notes				

Continued on page: _____

Project Type _____

Working Title _____

Date Started ____ / ____ / ____   **Date Completed** ____ / ____ / ____

File Location _____

Date	Time			Word Count	
	Start	Finish	Total	Start	Finish
			Total		Total

Word Count Goal _____ words   **Final Word Count** _____ words

Final Title _____

Final SubTitle _____

_____

_____

Total	Session Notes				

Continued on page: _____

Project Type _____

Working Title _____

Date Started ____ / ____ / ____   **Date Completed**   ____ / ____ / ____

File Location _____

Date	Time			Word Count	
	Start	**Finish**	**Total**	**Start**	**Finish**
			Total		Total

Word Count Goal _____ words **Final Word Count** _____ words

Final Title _____

Final SubTitle _____

_____

_____

Total	Session Notes				

Continued on page: _____

Project Type _____

Working Title _____

Date Started ___ / ___ / ___   **Date Completed** ___ / ___ / ___

File Location _____

Date	Time			Word Count	
	Start	Finish	Total	Start	Finish
			Total		Total

Word Count Goal _____ words **Final Word Count** _____ words
Final Title _____
Final SubTitle _____

_____
_____

Total	Session Notes				

97   Continued on page: _____

Project Type _____

Working Title _____

Date Started   ____ / ____ / ____   **Date Completed**   ____ / ____ / ____

File Location _____

| Date | Time | | | Word Count | |
	Start	Finish	Total	Start	Finish
			Total		Total

Word Count Goal _____ words **Final Word Count** _____ words

Final Title _____

Final SubTitle _____

_____

_____

Total	Session Notes				

  Continued on page: _____

Project Type _____

Working Title _____

Date Started ____ / ____ / ____   **Date Completed** ____ / ____ / ____

File Location _____

| Date | Time | | | Word Count | |
	Start	Finish	Total	Start	Finish
		Total			Total

Word Count Goal _____ words **Final Word Count** _____ words

Final Title _____

Final SubTitle _____

_____

_____

Total	Session Notes				

 Continued on page: _____

Project Type _____

Working Title _____

Date Started ____ / ____ / ____   **Date Completed** ____ / ____ / ____

File Location _____

Date	Time			Word Count	
	Start	Finish	Total	Start	Finish
			Total		Total

Word Count Goal _____ words   **Final Word Count** _____ words

Final Title _____

Final SubTitle _____

_____

_____

Total	Session Notes				

 Continued on page: _____

Project Type _____

Working Title _____

Date Started ____ / ____ / ____ **Date Completed** ____ / ____ / ____

File Location _____

| Date | Time | | | Word Count | |
	Start	Finish	Total	Start	Finish
		Total			Total

Word Count Goal _____ words **Final Word Count** _____ words

Final Title _____

Final SubTitle _____

_____

_____

Total	Session Notes				

 Continued on page: _____

Project Type _____

Working Title _____

Date Started ____ / ____ / ____   **Date Completed** ____ / ____ / ____

File Location _____

| Date | Time | | | Word Count | |
	Start	Finish	Total	Start	Finish
			Total		Total

Word Count Goal _____ words   **Final Word Count** _____ words

Final Title _____

Final SubTitle _____

_____

_____

Total	Session Notes				

Continued on page: _____

Project Type _____

Working Title _____

Date Started ___ / ___ / ___   **Date Completed** ___ / ___ / ___

File Location _____

Date	Time			Word Count	
	Start	**Finish**	**Total**	**Start**	**Finish**
			Total			Total

Word Count Goal _____ words **Final Word Count** _____ words

Final Title _____

Final SubTitle _____

_____

_____

Total	Session Notes				

 Continued on page: _____

Project Type _____

Working Title _____

Date Started ____ / ____ / ____   Date Completed   ____ / ____ / ____

File Location _____

Date	Time			Word Count	
	Start	Finish	Total	Start	Finish
			Total		Total

Word Count Goal _____ words **Final Word Count** _____ words

Final Title _____

Final SubTitle _____

_____

_____

Total	Session Notes				

 Continued on page: _____

Project Type _____

Working Title _____

Date Started ____ / ____ / ____   **Date Completed** ____ / ____ / ____

File Location _____

| Date | Time | | | Word Count | |
	Start	Finish	Total	Start	Finish
			Total		Total

Word Count Goal _____ words   **Final Word Count** _____ words

Final Title _____

Final SubTitle _____

_____

_____

Total	Session Notes				

 Continued on page: _____

Project Type _____

Working Title _____

Date Started ____ / ____ / ____   **Date Completed** ____ / ____ / ____

File Location _____

	Time			Word Count	
Date	**Start**	**Finish**	**Total**	**Start**	**Finish**
			Total		Total

Word Count Goal _____ words **Final Word Count** _____ words

Final Title _____

Final SubTitle _____

_____

_____

Total	Session Notes				

Continued on page: _____

Project Type _____

Working Title _____

Date Started ____ / ____ / ____   **Date Completed** ____ / ____ / ____

File Location _____

Date	Time			Word Count	
	Start	**Finish**	**Total**	**Start**	**Finish**
		Total			Total

Word Count Goal _____ words **Final Word Count** _____ words
Final Title _____
Final SubTitle _____

_____
_____

Total	Session Notes				

 Continued on page: _____

Project Type _____

Working Title _____

Date Started ____ / ____ / ____ **Date Completed** ____ / ____ / ____

File Location _____

	Time			Word Count	
Date	**Start**	**Finish**	**Total**	**Start**	**Finish**
		Total			Total

Word Count Goal _____ words   **Final Word Count** _____ words

Final Title _____

Final SubTitle _____

_____

_____

Total	Session Notes				

Continued on page: _____

Project Type _____

Working Title _____

Date Started ____ / ____ / ____ **Date Completed** ____ / ____ / ____

File Location _____

Date	Time			Word Count	
	Start	**Finish**	**Total**	**Start**	**Finish**
		Total			Total

Word Count Goal _____ words   **Final Word Count** _____ words

Final Title _____

Final SubTitle _____

_____

_____

Total	Session Notes				

 Continued on page: _____

Project Type _____

Working Title _____

Date Started ___ / ___ / ___   **Date Completed** ___ / ___ / ___

File Location _____

Date	Time			Word Count	
	Start	Finish	Total	Start	Finish
			Total			Total

Word Count Goal _____ words **Final Word Count** _____ words

Final Title _____

Final SubTitle _____

_____

_____

Total	Session Notes				

 Continued on page: _____

Project Type _____

Working Title _____

Date Started ____ / ____ / ____   **Date Completed** ____ / ____ / ____

File Location _____

Date	Time			Word Count	
	Start	Finish	Total	Start	Finish
			Total		Total

Word Count Goal _____ words **Final Word Count** _____ words

Final Title _____

Final SubTitle _____

_____

_____

Total	Session Notes				

 Continued on page: _____

Project Type _____

Working Title _____

Date Started ____ / ____ / ____ **Date Completed** ____ / ____ / ____

File Location _____

Date	Time			Word Count	
	Start	Finish	Total	Start	Finish
			Total			Total

Word Count Goal _____ words **Final Word Count** _____ words
Final Title _____
Final SubTitle _____
_____
_____

Total	Session Notes				

Continued on page: _____

Project Type _____

Working Title _____

Date Started ____ / ____ / ____   **Date Completed** ____ / ____ / ____

File Location _____

Date	Time			Word Count	
	Start	Finish	Total	Start	Finish
			Total		Total

Word Count Goal _____ words **Final Word Count** _____ words
Final Title _____
Final SubTitle _____

_____
_____

Total	Session Notes				

 Continued on page: _____

Project Type _____

Working Title _____

Date Started ____ / ____ / ____ **Date Completed** ____ / ____ / ____

File Location _____

Date	Time			Word Count	
	Start	Finish	Total	Start	Finish
			Total			Total

Word Count Goal _____ words **Final Word Count** _____ words

Final Title _____

Final SubTitle _____

_____

_____

Total	Session Notes				

 Continued on page: _____

Project Type _____

Working Title _____

Date Started ____ / ____ / ____   **Date Completed** ____ / ____ / ____

File Location _____

_____

| Date | Time | | | Word Count | |
	Start	Finish	Total	Start	Finish
			Total		Total

Word Count Goal _____ words   **Final Word Count** _____ words

Final Title _____

Final SubTitle _____

_____

_____

Total	Session Notes				

 Continued on page: _____

Project Type _____

Working Title _____

Date Started ____ / ____ / ____   **Date Completed** ____ / ____ / ____

File Location _____

| Date | Time | | | Word Count | |
	Start	Finish	Total	Start	Finish
		Total			Total

Word Count Goal _____ words   **Final Word Count** _____ words

Final Title _____

Final SubTitle _____

_____

_____

Total	Session Notes				

 Continued on page: _____

Project Type _____

Working Title _____

Date Started ____ / ____ / ____   **Date Completed** ____ / ____ / ____

File Location _____

Date	Time			Word Count	
	Start	Finish	Total	Start	Finish
			Total		Total

Word Count Goal _____ words   **Final Word Count** _____ words

Final Title _____

Final SubTitle _____

_____

_____

Total	Session Notes				

 Continued on page: _____

Project Type _____

Working Title _____

Date Started ___ / ___ / ___ **Date Completed** ___ / ___ / ___

File Location _____

Date	Time			Word Count	
	Start	Finish	Total	Start	Finish
			Total		Total

Word Count Goal _____ words   **Final Word Count** _____ words

Final Title _____

Final SubTitle _____

_____

_____

Total	Session Notes				

 Continued on page: _____

Project Type _____

Working Title _____

Date Started ___ / ___ / ___ **Date Completed** ___ / ___ / ___

File Location _____

Date	Time			Word Count	
	Start	Finish	Total	Start	Finish
			Total		Total

Word Count Goal _____ words **Final Word Count** _____ words

Final Title _____

Final SubTitle _____

_____

_____

Total	Session Notes				

 Continued on page: _____

Project Type _____

Working Title _____

Date Started   ____ / ____ / ____   **Date Completed**   ____ / ____ / ____

File Location _____

	Time			Word Count	
Date	**Start**	**Finish**	**Total**	**Start**	**Finish**
			Total		Total

Word Count Goal _____ words **Final Word Count** _____ words

Final Title _____

Final SubTitle _____

_____

_____

Total	Session Notes				

 Continued on page: _____

Project Type _____

Working Title _____

Date Started ____ / ____ / ____   **Date Completed** ____ / ____ / ____

File Location _____

| Date | Time | | | Word Count | |
	Start	Finish	Total	Start	Finish
			Total		Total

Word Count Goal _____ words   **Final Word Count** _____ words
Final Title _____
Final SubTitle _____
_____
_____

Total	Session Notes				

 Continued on page: _____

Project Type _____

Working Title _____

Date Started ___ / ___ / ___   **Date Completed** ___ / ___ / ___

File Location _____

	Time			Word Count	
Date	Start	Finish	Total	Start	Finish
		Total			Total

Word Count Goal _____ words   **Final Word Count** _____ words

Final Title _____

Final SubTitle _____

_____

_____

Total	Session Notes				

 Continued on page: _____

Project Type _____

Working Title _____

Date Started ____ / ____ / ____   **Date Completed** ____ / ____ / ____

File Location _____

Date	Time			Word Count	
	Start	Finish	Total	Start	Finish
			Total		Total

Word Count Goal _____ words **Final Word Count** _____ words
Final Title _____
Final SubTitle _____

_____

_____

Total	Session Notes				

Continued on page: _____

Project Type _____

Working Title _____

Date Started ___ / ___ / ___   **Date Completed** ___ / ___ / ___

File Location _____

Date	Time			Word Count	
	Start	Finish	Total	Start	Finish
			Total		Total

Word Count Goal _____ words **Final Word Count** _____ words

Final Title _____

Final SubTitle _____

_____

_____

Total	Session Notes				

 Continued on page: _____

eDiY Publishing

Other Books

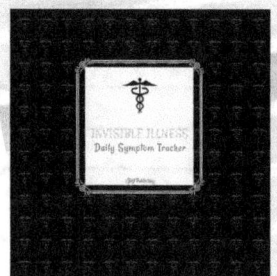

Invisible Illness: Daily Symptoms Tracker

Fibromyalgia CFS ME MS Cancer: Daily Symptoms Tracker

Published Books Tracker for Self Publishing Authors